HOW TO DRAW FANTASY
ORCS, ELVES AND DWARVES

Steve Beaumont

W
FRANKLIN WATTS
LONDON · SYDNEY

First published in 2007 by Franklin Watts

Copyright © 2007 Arcturus Publishing Limited

Franklin Watts
338 Euston Road
London NW1 3BH

Franklin Watts Australia
Level 17/207 Kent St, Sydney, NSW 2000

Produced by Arcturus Publishing Limited,
26/27 Bickels Yard, 151–153 Bermondsey Street, London SE1 3HA

The right of Steve Beaumont to be identified as the author of this work has been asserted by him in accordance with the Copyright, Designs and Patents Act 1988.

Artwork and text: Steve Beaumont
Editor: Alex Woolf
Designer: Jane Hawkins

A CIP catalogue record for this book is available from the British Library.

Dewey Decimal Classification Number: 743'.87

ISBN: 978 0 7496 7653 7

Printed in China

Franklin Watts is a division of Hachette Children's Books.

Contents

INTRODUCTION	4
EQUIPMENT	6
FACES	8
DWARF	10
WARRIOR ORC	14
GOBLIN ORC	18
FEMALE ELF	22
MALE ELF	26
GLOSSARY	30
FURTHER INFORMATION	31
INDEX	32

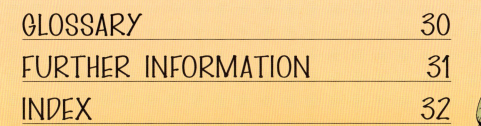

Introduction

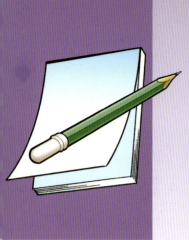

If you've picked up this book, you are probably a big fan of sword-and-sorcery movies, books or games. You may be one of those fans who enjoys the genre so much that you'd like to have a go at creating some magical characters for yourself. If so, this book will help you get started on the right path.

One of the best things about drawing dwarves, orcs, elves and other fantasy figures is that – apart from the basic rules of anatomy and perspective – there are no other rules. In fantasy art, no one can tell you that a character's nose is too long or her ears are too pointy – these are products of your imagination and you can draw them exactly as you please!

Dwarves

Although short in stature, a dwarf is a fierce and valiant warrior on the battlefield. Dwarves originally came from Norse folklore and mythology, so are often shown as miniature Vikings. They are distantly related to elves and many have magic powers.

Elves
Elves are mystical creatures, usually pictured as young-looking men and women of great beauty, who live in forests, underground, or in wells and springs. Despite their graceful appearance, elves can be fierce warriors when they have to defend their kingdom against enemies, such as dragons and orcs. Many of them possess magic powers.

Orcs
Although basically human in shape, orcs are mean, ugly and aggressive characters. But despite their unpleasantness – or perhaps because of it! – they certainly are fun to draw – as you'll find out.

Equipment

To start with, you'll need the tools of the trade. Decent materials and equipment are essential if you want to produce high-quality illustrations.

Paper

For your practice sketches, buy some cheap A4 or A3 paper from a stationery shop. When practising ink drawing, use line art paper, which can be purchased from an art or craft shop.

For painting with watercolours, use watercolour paper. Most art shops stock a large range of weights and sizes – 250 g/m or 300 g/m is fine.

Pencils

Get a good range of lead pencils ranging from soft (6B) to hard (2H). Hard-leaded pencils last longer and leave fewer smudges on your paper. Soft-leaded ones leave darker marks on the paper and wear down more quickly. 2H pencils are a good medium-range product to start with.

For fine, detailed work, mechanical pencils are ideal. These are available in a range of lead thicknesses, 0.5 mm being a good middle range.

Pens

For inking, use either a ballpoint or a simple dip pen and nib. For colouring, experiment with the wide variety of felt-tips on the market.

Markers
These are very versatile pens that, with practice, can give very pleasing results.

Brushes
Some artists like to use a fine brush for inking line work. This takes a bit more practice to master, but the results can be very satisfying. If you want to try your hand at brushwork, you will need some good-quality sable brushes.

Watercolours and gouache
Most art shops will also stock a wide range of these products from student to professional quality.

Inks
Any good brand will do.

Eraser
There are three types of eraser: rubber, plastic and putty. Try all three to see which you prefer.

Oh, and you may need something for sharpening your pencils…

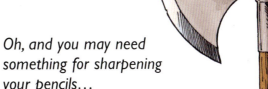

Faces

As with all character drawing, so much of the personality of a dwarf, orc or elf is to be found in the face. It's therefore worth spending a bit of time honing your techniques in this crucial area.

Constructing the face

The human head generally fits into a square. Note that the nose and chin protrude slightly. It may help to divide the square into quarters. The eyes generally sit halfway above the centre line, with the nose taking up half the depth of the bottom square. Note the alignment of the ears in relation to the eyes and nose. This example is based on a standard-sized head – of course, with fantasy drawing, it may be necessary to adjust this formula.

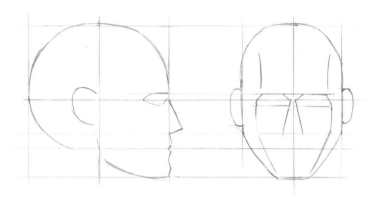

Elves

Note the refined, slender features of this delicate fantasy race. Note also that our elf is looking down and a little to the side, rather than face on, so draw your guidelines with a curve, as though you were constructing a 3D object.

Dwarves

These guys have shorter, wider heads than the average human head shown on the previous page, but let's not forget that dwarves are just as important as human warriors in fantasy art, so make sure they have a charm all of their own.

Orcs

Let's take a look at this classic brute. Observe the big head and low forehead (indicators of the very small brain inside), and don't forget the mouth full of sharp teeth. What a charmer!

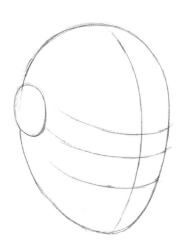

Here we have a smaller, thinner variation on the face above, featuring a hooked nose and beady eyes, giving this beast an even more sinister appearance.

Dwarf

In this exercise, we'll try drawing a dwarf in an action pose. Remember that, although short, dwarves are strong, and well capable of wielding a heavy battleaxe. To give a sense of his power, we'll give him a wide stance and place his head low, in line with his shoulders.

Stage 1
Start with a stick figure to establish the basic shape. Don't forget – this is a dwarf, so your stick man may, in fact, appear more like a stick child.

Stage 2
Add body shape to the stick figure. The human form can be constructed from geometric shapes such as cylinders and spheres. Use these to create the dwarf's torso and limbs.

Stage 3
Now put in the facial features, including the beard. Add the outer body form over the geometric shapes. Finish his head by crowning him with a helmet.

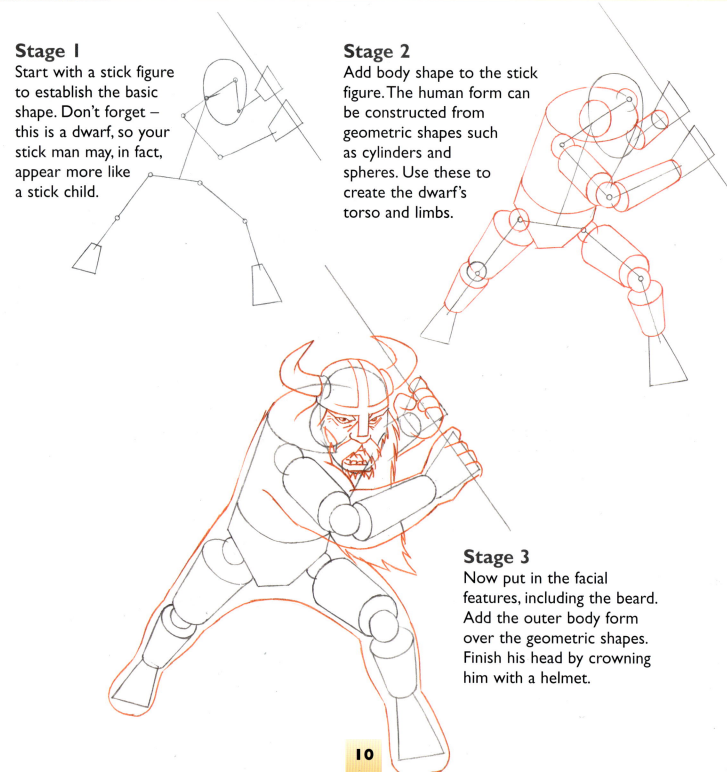

Stage 4
Erase the geometric shapes, and then it's time to armour up. Let's give him a big axe to wield and kit him out with some protective armour and a cloak.

Stage 5
Clean up the line work, add some shading to the clothes and the axe to give them more solidity, and add any detail that you feel may enhance the drawing – but don't overdo it.

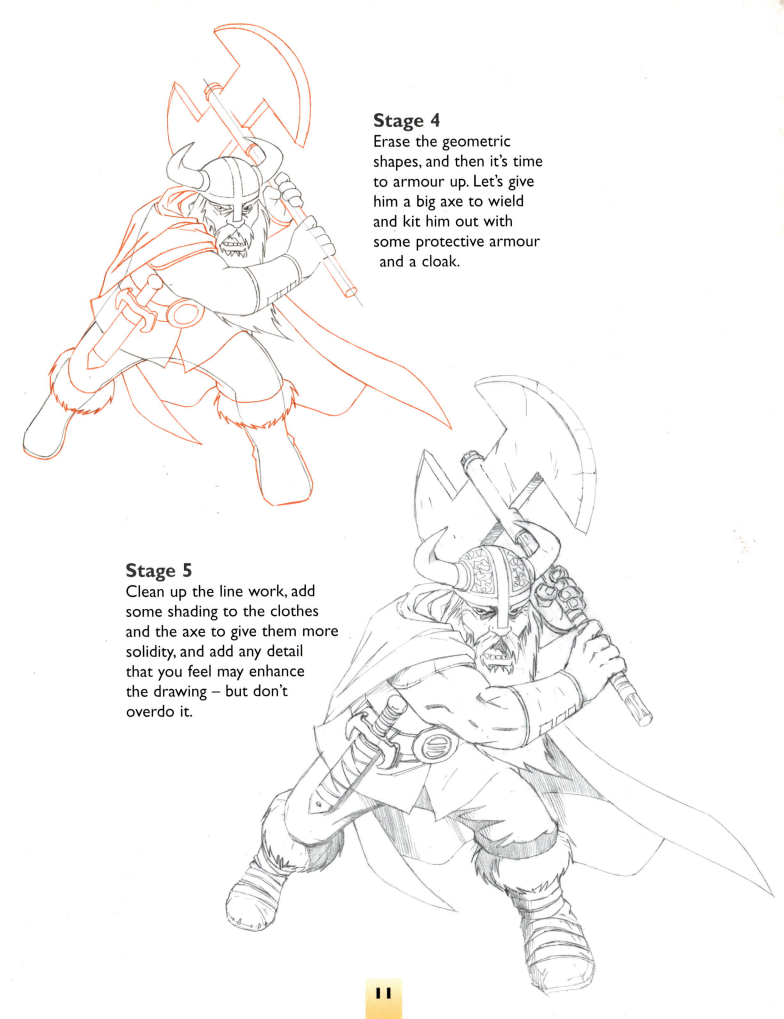

Stage 6
Okay, now let's start inking him in – be careful not to over-ink the beard. Add hair to his arms and detail to his horned helmet.

Stage 7
Complete the inking of the dwarf's lower half, taking care with the leather binding of his boots.

Stage 8
You can colour your drawing, if you like, using marker pens, felt-tips or watercolours. Lay down each colour in one continuous wash if you can, applying the colour as smoothly as possible. Ginger is always a popular choice for dwarf hair, but experiment with your own ideas. Keeping to masculine colours, such as dark browns and greys, will add strength and weight to your drawing.

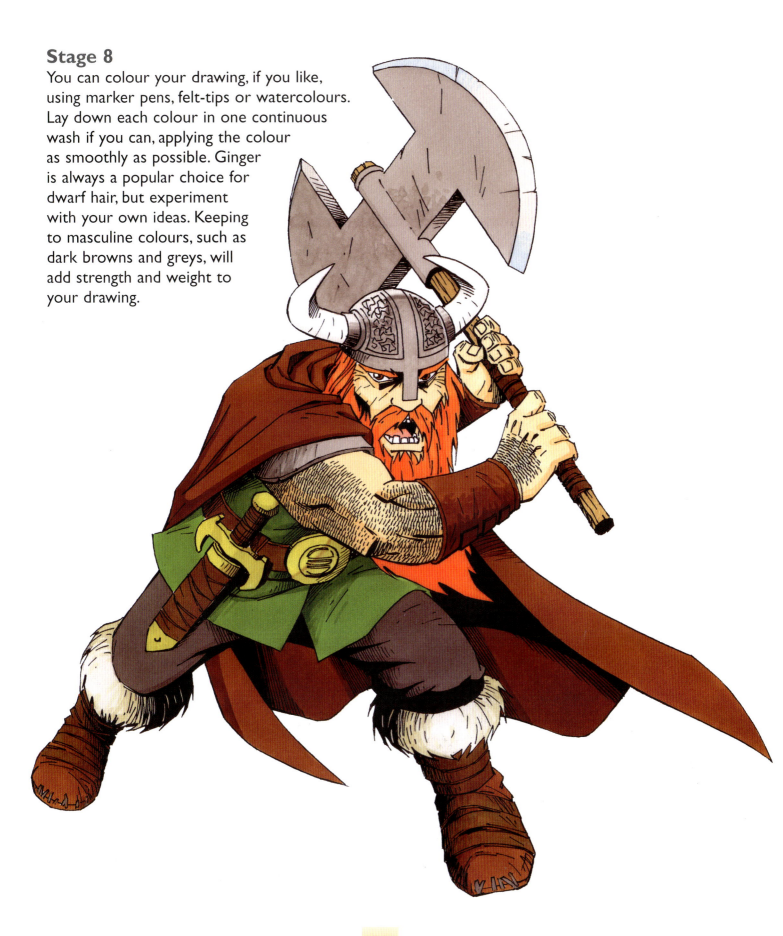

Warrior Orc

No one really knows the true origins of orcs, only that a force of evil created them. This one's a real baddy!

Stage 1
Start with the stick figure. Orcs are generally taller than adult humans. Bear this in mind when sketching your figure.

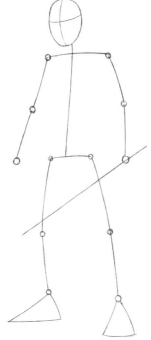

Stage 2
Apply the geometric shapes. Orcs are far more bulky and muscular than humans, so go for fatter and broader shapes.

Stage 3
Give him a facial expression. Remember, this is an orc, so make him ugly – it's okay to go over the top here. Add the outer body form over the geometric shapes.

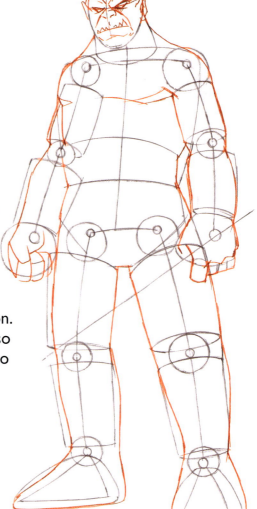

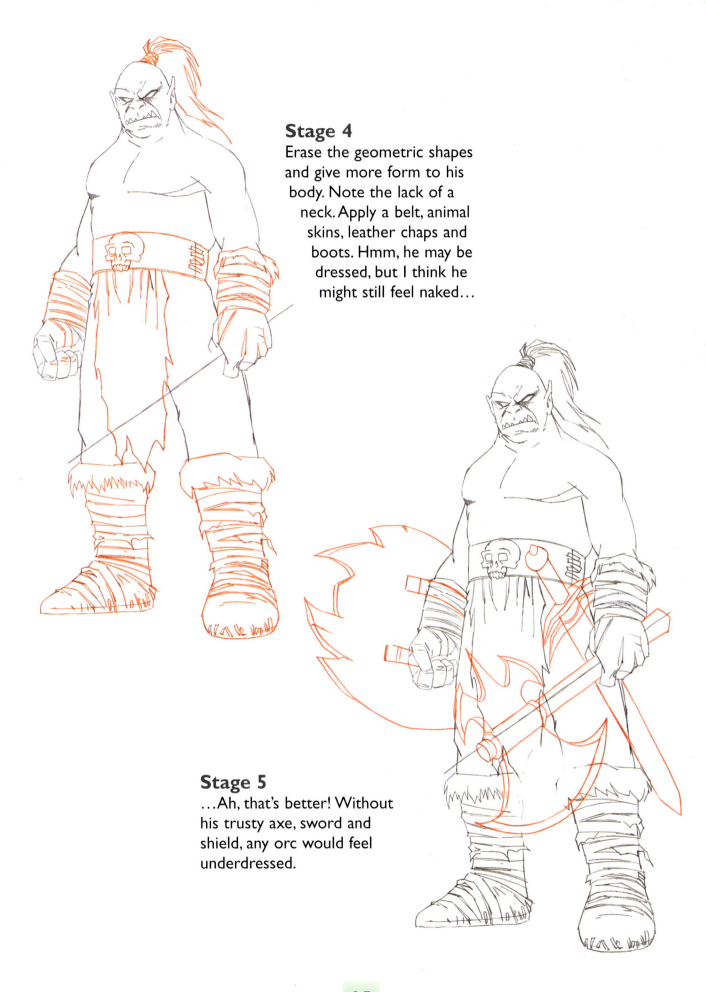

Stage 4
Erase the geometric shapes and give more form to his body. Note the lack of a neck. Apply a belt, animal skins, leather chaps and boots. Hmm, he may be dressed, but I think he might still feel naked…

Stage 5
…Ah, that's better! Without his trusty axe, sword and shield, any orc would feel underdressed.

Stage 6
Tidy up the pencil sketch, getting rid of any unwanted detail. Add shading to give the orc shape and form.

Stage 7
Now you can make a start on the inking.

Stage 8
Try not to overdo the inking, or you'll risk spoiling the more detailed areas.

Stage 9

If you decide to colour your drawing, remember that orc skin tends to be dull – muddy greys and browns with a green hue. Stick to muted colours for the armour and weapons, too.

Goblin Orc

Orcs come in all shapes and sizes, and here we have a small goblin-type orc who's just as deadly as his larger cousins. It is believed that the various types of orc came about through selective breeding. Some were thought to be a combination of elf and pig or wolf. With this character we have a bit of all three, with elf ears, a pig face, and the mane and legs of a wolf.

Stage 1
Try to think of this stick figure as a mix of human and animal forms. Note that the legs are rather like those of a dog.

Stage 2
Add some geometric shapes to bulk out the goblin orc's form.

Stage 3
The facial features differ considerably from those of the warrior orc in the previous exercise. This one has a thinner face, bigger eyes and larger ears. Note that the eyes are left blank. There is no pupil, which makes the overall appearance more sinister.

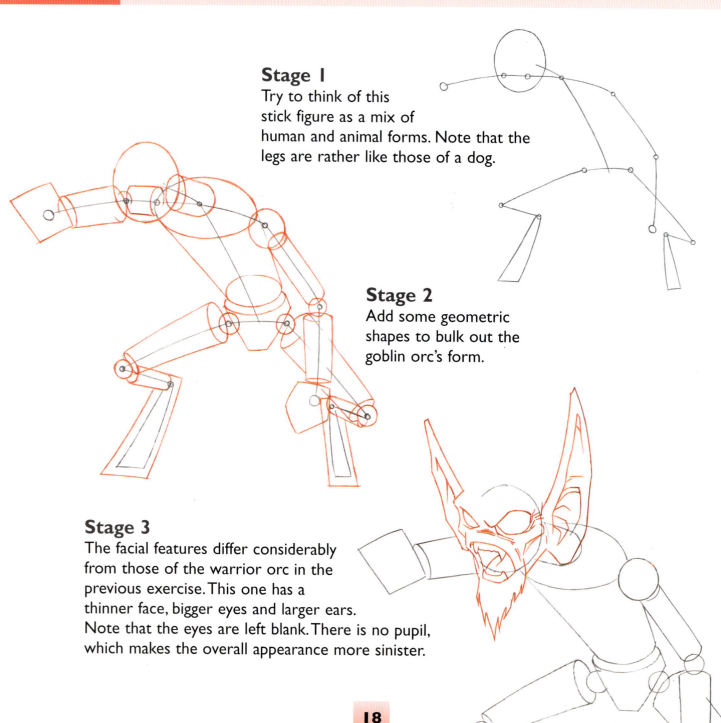

Stage 4
Now add the outer body form, and shape the claws and talons. Place a heavy club in his fist. Use jagged lines to give him a partly hairy outline. Give the orc a big shaggy mane so he looks like a kind of demonic punk rocker.

Stage 5
Now erase the geometric shapes and add shading and highlights to give him depth and solidity.

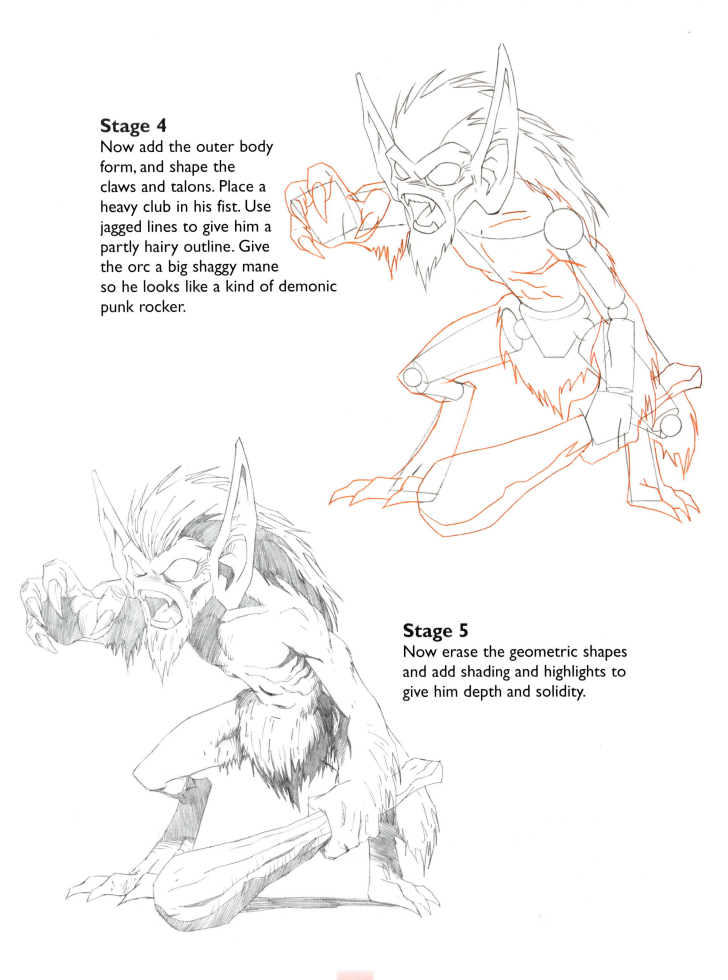

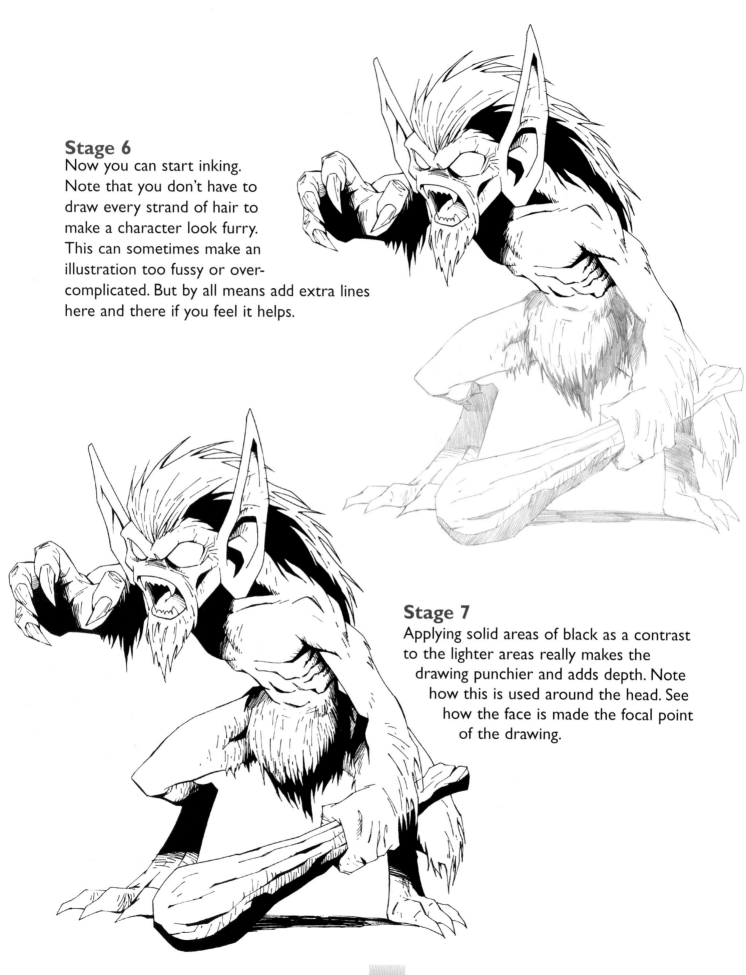

Stage 6
Now you can start inking. Note that you don't have to draw every strand of hair to make a character look furry. This can sometimes make an illustration too fussy or over-complicated. But by all means add extra lines here and there if you feel it helps.

Stage 7
Applying solid areas of black as a contrast to the lighter areas really makes the drawing punchier and adds depth. Note how this is used around the head. See how the face is made the focal point of the drawing.

Stage 8

Orcs are generally dull and dirty-looking in colour. Applying these tones helps to create a more sinister appearance. Of course, you can also experiment with your own colour schemes – but remember, anything too light and bright may make this character less scary.

Female Elf

This is a classic female elf. She possesses extraordinary beauty, with big, expressive eyes, graceful, fragile features, pointed ears and high cheekbones.

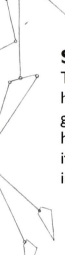

Stage 1
This elf will be hovering above the ground, so draw her stick frame as if she's floating in space.

Stage 2
Add geometric shapes to the stick figure.

Stage 3
Now draw in her outline. When drawing elves, care must be taken to give them smooth, elegant features.

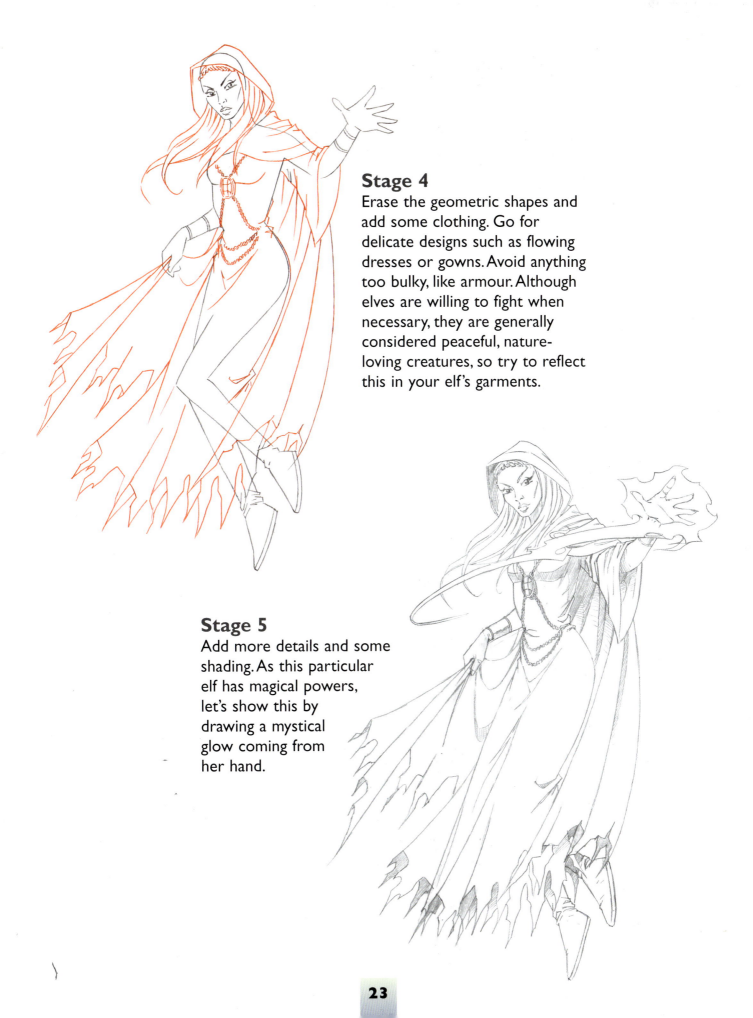

Stage 4
Erase the geometric shapes and add some clothing. Go for delicate designs such as flowing dresses or gowns. Avoid anything too bulky, like armour. Although elves are willing to fight when necessary, they are generally considered peaceful, nature-loving creatures, so try to reflect this in your elf's garments.

Stage 5
Add more details and some shading. As this particular elf has magical powers, let's show this by drawing a mystical glow coming from her hand.

Stage 6
Tidy up the pencil work, add any small details you feel may enhance the drawing and begin the inking.

Stage 7
When inking females, a good tip is to refrain from using too much heavy linework. Keep it light and delicate.

Stage 8
If you want to apply colour, remember that elves are generally woodland dwellers, so pick a colour scheme that reflects this. Greens and yellows are a good choice.

Male Elf

Elves are generally smaller than adult humans and it's often difficult to distinguish between male and female elves at first glance. So when producing drawings of them, you may find yourself using the same shapes and forms. Note that male elves don't have any beard growth.

Stage 1
Our elf is an expert archer, about to fire an arrow, so create the stick figure in low stance.

Stage 2
Now give form to the stick figure. Use slightly more bulky geometric shapes than the ones used to create the female elf.

Stage 3
Add refined, delicate features to the face.

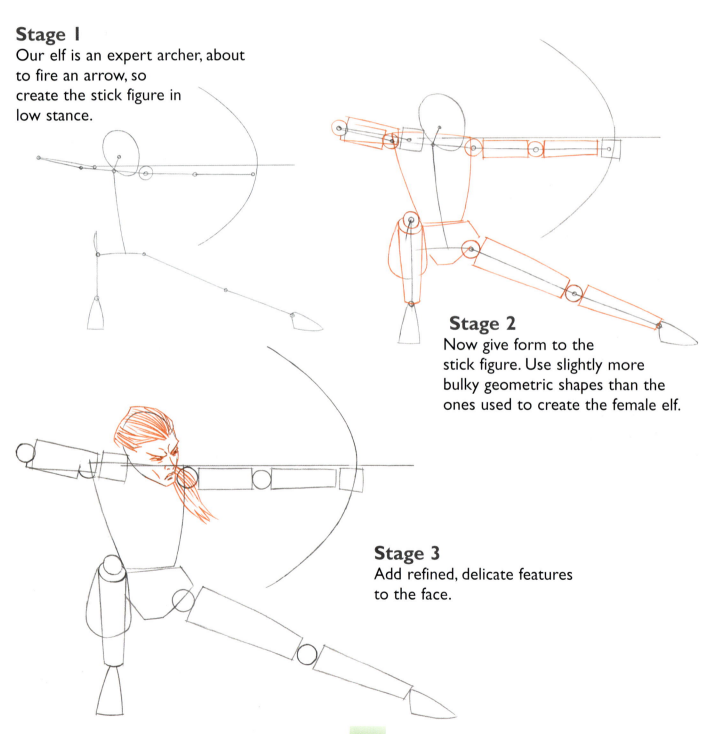

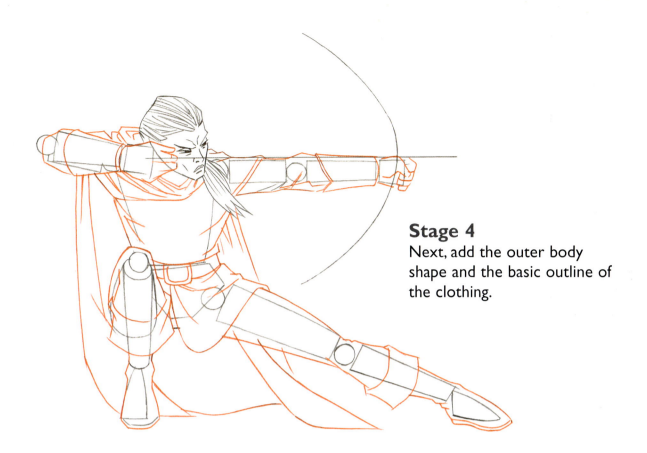

Stage 4
Next, add the outer body shape and the basic outline of the clothing.

Stage 5
Erase the geometric shapes and dress the elf in fine garments, with a hooded cape to complete the forest-dweller look.

Stage 6
Refine your pencil work and add some shading to give your elf solidity. Note that even his bow and arrow are drawn in a refined way, in keeping with his overall elfin appearance.

Stage 7
Start applying ink, using fine lines.

Stage 8
Note that large solid areas are kept to a minimum to keep the image light.

Stage 9
Again, greens are the obvious choice, but perhaps go for dark olive tones with splashes of brown thrown in, as this is a male elf.

Glossary

alignment The positioning of different parts of an object or objects relative to each other.

anatomy The physical structure of a human or other organism.

dwarf A fantasy creature of short stature with a human appearance.

chaps Protective leather leggings.

cylinder A shape with straight sides and circular ends of equal size.

elf A fantasy creature of graceful appearance, similar to a human being, and often considered to have magical powers.

elfin Like an elf.

facial *adjective* Of the face.

focal point The part of a picture to which an observer's eye is drawn.

geometric shape Simple shapes, such as cubes, spheres and cylinders.

goblin A fantasy creature of unpleasant appearance and a usually evil or mischievous personality.

gouache A mixture of non-transparent watercolour paint and gum.

highlight An area of very light tone in an illustration that provides contrast or the appearance of illumination.

mechanical pencil A pencil with replaceable lead that may be advanced as needed.

mystical Something with supernatural or spiritual significance or power.

mythology The myths that relate to a particular culture, telling of their ancestors, heroes, gods and other supernatural beings.

Norse Relating to ancient or medieval Scandinavia, especially Norway.

orc A member of an imaginary race of ugly, warlike and evil creatures.

perspective In drawing, changing the relative size and appearance of objects to allow for the effects of distance.

refined Graceful and elegant.

sable brush An artist's brush made with the hairs of a sable, a small mammal from northern Asia.

sinister Threatening or menacing.

sphere An object shaped like a ball.

stance The way a person stands.

stick figure A simple drawing of a person with single lines for the torso, arms and legs.

tone Any of the possible shades of a particular colour.

torso The upper part of the human body, not including the head and arms.

valiant Brave and steadfast.

Vikings A seafaring people from Scandinavia, who carried out raids and invasions on parts of north-western Europe from the 8th to 11th centuries AD.

watercolour Paint made by mixing pigments (substances that give something its colour) with water.

Further Information

Books

Drawing and Painting Fantasy Figures: From the Imagination to the Page by Finlay Cowan (David and Charles, 2004)

How to Draw Fairies and Mermaids by Fiona Watt and Jan McCafferty (illustrator) (Usborne, 2005)

How to Draw Fantasy Characters by Christopher Hart (Watson-Guptill Publications, 1999)

How to Draw Ghosts, Goblins, Witches and other Spooky Characters by Barbara Soloff Levy (Sagebrush, 1999)

How to Draw Wizards, Dragons and other Magical Creatures by Barbara Soloff Levy (Dover Publications, 2004)

Kids Draw Angels, Elves, Fairies and More by Christopher Hart (Watson-Guptill, 2001)

Websites

akari-paws.tripod.com/id126.html
A tutorial on drawing elves and fairies.

drawsketch.about.com/od/drawfantasyandscifi/tp/imagination.htm
Advice on drawing from the imagination.

www.elfeyes.com/art/art.html
A gallery of elf art.

elfwood.lysator.liu.se/farp/art.html
An online guide to creating your own fantasy art.

Note to parents and teachers:

Every effort has been made by the publishers to ensure that these websites are suitable for children and contain no inappropriate or offensive material. However, because of the nature of the Internet, it is impossible to guarantee that the contents of these sites will not be altered. We strongly advise that Internet access is supervised by a responsible adult.

Index

A
anatomy 4, 30
animal forms 18
animal skins 15
armour 11, 17, 23
arms 12
axe 10, 11, 15

B
beard 10, 12, 26
body shape 10, 14, 15, 16, 18, 19, 26, 27
boots 12, 15
bow and arrow 26, 28

C
cape 27
chaps 15, 30
chin 8
claws 19
cloak 11
clothing 11, 23, 27
club 19
colouring 13, 17, 21, 25, 29
contrast 20
cylinders 10, 30

D
dip pens and nibs 6
dwarves 4, 8, 9, 10–13, 30

E
ears 8, 18, 22
egg shapes
elves 4, 5, 8, 18, 22–29, 30
equipment 6–7
eyes 8, 9, 18, 22

F
face 8–9, 18, 20
facial expressions 14
facial features 10, 18, 22, 26
felt-tips 6, 13
female elf 22–25, 26

G
geometric shapes 10, 14, 15, 18, 19, 22, 23, 26, 27, 30
goblin orc 18–21

H
hair 12, 13, 20
hands 23
head 8, 9, 10, 20
helmet 10, 12
highlights 19, 30
humans 5, 8, 9, 14, 18, 26

I
inking 6, 12, 16, 20, 24, 28, 29

M
magic powers 4, 5, 23
male elf 26–29
mane 18, 19
marker pens 7, 13
mechanical pencils 6, 30

N
nose 8, 9

O
orcs 4, 5, 8, 9, 14–21, 30
outline 19, 22

P
pencil work 16, 24, 28
perspective 4, 30

S
shading 11, 16, 19, 20, 23, 28
shield 15
shoulders 10
skin 17
spheres 10, 30
stick figure 10, 14, 18, 22, 26, 30
sword 15

T
talons 19
teeth 9
torso 10, 30

W
warrior orc 14–17, 18
warriors 4, 5, 9
watercolours 6, 7, 13, 30